T0419676

FLY GUY PRESENTS: GARBAGE & RECYCLING

Tedd Arnold

Scholastic Inc.

For Angelo Bruno and Eddie Nieves, sanitation workers in Manhattan's West Village, whose StoryCorps story inspired me!

Thank you to the following for their contributions to this book: AnnMarie Anderson; Monica G. Devincenzi, municipal relationship manager, Republic Services; Tim Flanagan, general manager, Monterey Regional Waste Management District; and Christopher Sauve, deputy commissioner, City of Chicago.

Photos @: cover: Rokas Tenys/Shutterstock; back cover: Jim West/Alamy Stock Photo; 4–5: Ralph125/iStockphoto; 6 top left: worradirek/Shutterstock; 6 top right: bgfoto/iStockphoto; 6 bottom left: photka/Shutterstock; 6 bottom right: Michael Neelon/Alamy Stock Photo; 7 top: Juanmonino/iStockphoto; 7 bottom: Walter Zerla/Blend Images/Media Bakery; 8 top: Mike Kleist/Dreamstime; 8 bottom: Gilbert S. Grant/Science Source; 9: neenawat/iStockphoto; 10 top: Tom Beelmann/Media Bakery; 10 bottom: Jim West/Alamy Stock Photo; 11 top: Alan Schein/Getty Images; 11 bottom: LesPalenik/Shutterstock; 12 top: PJF Military Collection/Alamy Stock Photo; 12 bottom: Paul Vasarhelyi/Shutterstock; 13 truck: B Christopher/Alamy Stock Photo; 13 background: chinasong/Shutterstock; 14 top: Tom Uhlman/Alamy Stock Photo; 14 bottom: PeopleImages/iStockphoto; 15 top: kzenon/iStockphoto; 15 bottom: Sigrid Gombert/age fotostock; 16 top: Lulub/Shutterstock; 16 bottom left: Andrew Lichtenstein/Getty Images; 16 bottom right: ZUMA Press, Inc./Alamy Stock Photo; 17 top: Dave and Les Jacobs/Getty Images; 17 center: Kanawa_Studio/iStockphoto; 17 bottom: Marina Lohrbach/Shutterstock; 18 top: Sorin Alb/Shutterstock; 18 bottom: View Stock/Alamy Stock Photo; 19 left: David Grossman/Alamy Stock Photo; 19 right: Blulz60/iStockphoto; 20 top: Richard Thomas/Dreamstime; 20 bottom left: Dechev/Dreamstime; 20 bottom right: MawardiBahar/Shutterstock; 21 left: Juice Images/Alamy Stock Photo; 21 right: Ermess/Dreamstime; 22 top: Chip Chipman/Bloomberg/Getty Images; 22 bottom: Echo/Getty Images; 23 top: Joerg Boethling/Alamy Stock Photo; 23 center: RGB Ventures/SuperStock/Alamy Stock Photo; 23 bottom: ASK Images/Alamy Stock Photo; 24 left: Juice Images/Alamy Stock Photo; 24 right: Jo Kirchherr Image Source/Newscom; 25 top left: Chris Pearsall/Alamy Stock Photo; 25 top right: Bowribbee/Shutterstock; 25 bottom left: lepas2004/iStockphoto; 25 bottom right: DPD ImageStock/Alamy Stock Photo; 26 top: Evan Lorne/Shutterstock; 26 bottom: Anna Hoychuk/Shutterstock; 27 left: Education Images/Getty Images; 27 right: Richard Levine/Alamy Stock Photo; 28 top: Utopia_88/iStockphoto; 28 bottom: Jonathan Alcorn/ZUMAPRESS/Newscom; 29 top left: Paulo Oliveira/Alamy Stock Photo; 29 top right: Akulinina/Shutterstock; 29 bottom: Paulo Oliveira/Alamy Stock Photo; 30 top: Tetra Images/Alamy Stock Photo; 30 center: ktkusmtku/Shutterstock; 30 bottom: B Christopher/Alamy Stock Photo.

Library of Congress Cataloging-in-Publication Data available

ISBN 978-1-338-21719-3

16 15 14 13 12 11   23

Printed in the U.S.A.   40
First printing, March 2019

Book design by Marissa Asuncion

A boy had a pet fly named Fly Guy.
Fly Guy could say the boy's name —

"I have a special treat for you, Fly Guy," Buzz said.
"Today we are visiting a landfill!"

YEZZ!

Fly Guy loved garbage!
He and Buzz couldn't wait to learn more
about trash . . .

Trash from homes, schools, and businesses is called municipal (myoo-NIS-uh-puhl) solid waste. Here are some examples of things that make up municipal waste.

FOODZ!?!

PAPER

LEAVES AND GRASS

METAL

PLASTIC AND GLASS

A city's sanitation (san-i-TAY-shun) department or a local garbage company is responsible for collecting, recycling, and discarding these materials. In the United States, people throw away over 250 million tons of trash each year—more than any other country.

Most of that trash ends up in the country's 2,000 or so landfills.

Landfills are areas where garbage is discarded. A landfill starts as a large hole in the ground covered with clay soil and a plastic liner. This keeps waste from getting into the soil and groundwater underneath.

Giant landfill compactors crush and pack down trash. Then, the garbage is covered with a thin layer of soil. Over time, tiny organisms called bacteria eat the trash, causing it to decompose (dee-kuhm-POHZ), or break down.

YUMZEE!

The bacteria in a landfill also cause several gases to form—including one very stinky gas called hydrogen sulfide. This gas smells like rotten eggs! It is so stinky, humans can detect it even in tiny amounts. That's why trash sometimes stinks!

A fly can smell garbage from almost five miles away!

Sanitation departments and garbage companies around the country collect waste using 130,000 garbage and recycling trucks.

These trucks haul the waste to landfills and recycling plants. A typical garbage truck can haul around 20,000 pounds of trash.

Some garbage trucks use diesel fuel.

Others run on a natural gas created from landfill gases. Natural gas is less expensive and better for the environment.

Many trucks have mechanical arms. Controls inside the truck are used to grab, lift, and dump containers of trash into the top of the truck.

Other garbage trucks are rear loaders. This means that garbage is dumped into the back of the truck. Then a shovel-like wall pushes the trash further inside. The *crunch* sound you hear is the trash being squished to make more room!

PACKER PANEL

TAILGATE

GRAB HANDLE

LOADING HOPPER

LOADING SILL

RIDING STEP

Sanitation workers have very dangerous jobs. Lifting heavy containers of trash can cause injuries. Workers might touch something harmful in the trash, such as broken glass or dangerous chemicals. And sanitation workers often ride standing on the outside of their trucks, so a crash with another vehicle can be deadly.

Sanitation workers' uniforms help to keep them safe. They wear gloves and boots for protection. And their outermost layer of clothing helps make sanitation workers more visible to other drivers.

Once there is no more space in a landfill, it is covered and closed.

This land used to be a landfill. The machine continues to vent gases that form beneath the surface.

Sometimes this land is later turned into a park, a golf course, or even a ski resort!

But what happens to the garbage that doesn't get sent to a landfill?

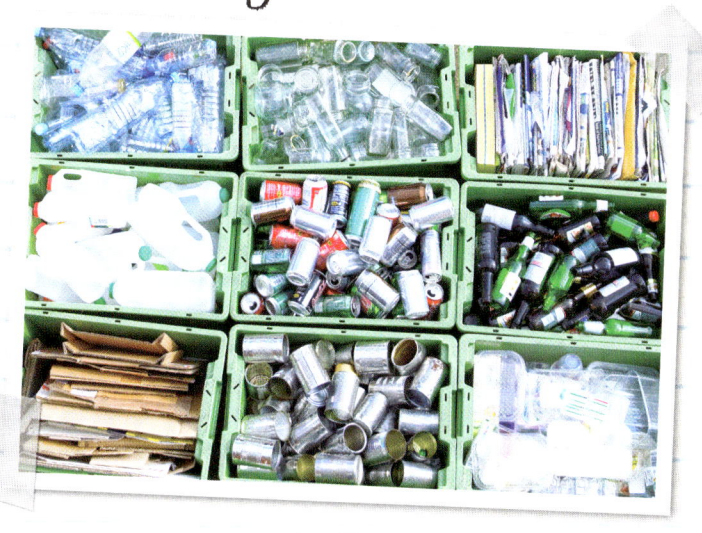

In the United States, the rest of our trash is recycled or turned into soil through composting.

In the United States, state and local governments make their own recycling laws. Starting a recycling program can be expensive. But recycling can save money—and the environment— in the long run.

Recycling programs are expanding. Right now, 25 states have laws that say certain electronics, called e-waste, must be recycled. Laws like these are important because many electronics contain toxic materials that can be harmful when they end up in landfills.

This is America Recycles Day!

15 NOVEMBER

Most metal, paper, plastic, and glass can be recycled.

Rubber tires and lead-acid batteries used in vehicles can be recycled, too.

But some items like lightbulbs and dishes cannot be recycled. Plastics like potato chip bags and plastic wrap cannot be recycled either. E-waste must be carefully recycled through special programs. Televisions, phones, and refrigerators are all e-waste.

COMPUTER AND PRINTER E-WASTE.

SIGH

CORN CHIPS

TRASH

When a truck arrives at a recycling center, its contents are dumped out.

Then recyclables are moved to a conveyer belt.

Everything is separated, and trash that was mixed in by mistake is removed.

Similar materials are crushed, compacted, and tied up in huge cubes called bales.

Then the bales are transported to different plants for processing before being made into new products.

Each bale of paper or cardboard saves about 15 trees!

Let's follow a bale of plastic bottles to a plastics recycling facility!

A forklift breaks up the bale and drops it onto a conveyer belt. The bottles are prewashed and sorted by color.

Next, the bottles are washed and heated to remove labels and bottle caps.

RECYCLING MAP

The bottles are ground into flakes. Then they are washed again and dried. The flakes are melted and made into tiny plastic pellets.

These plastic pellets can be used to make new things. Carpets, fleece jackets, and park benches can all be made from recycled plastic. New plastic bottles can be made, too!

NIZE FLEEZE!

Natural materials like fruits and vegetables, eggshells, and leaves take up a lot of space in landfills. But they can be recycled through composting.

This process breaks down food and yard waste into a rich soil for gardens and yards in just two to four months.

Some people compost in their backyards. But some cities like San Francisco and New York are beginning to pick up this waste along with trash and recycling. This helps reduce the amount of trash in landfills.

A typical American family throws away $1,300 of food in one year!

Unfortunately, some trash doesn't get disposed of properly. This litter ends up in our lakes, rivers, and oceans.

When plastic trash ends up in the ocean, it breaks down into confetti-sized pieces.

Ocean currents have pushed millions of these plastic bits together in one part of the Pacific Ocean called the Great Pacific Garbage Patch.

Water sample from the Great Pacific Garbage Patch

Birds and marine animals think the plastic is food and eat it. The plastic can make the animals sick.

If you like to eat fish, you might find yourself eating our oceans' plastic trash one day, too!

NAZZTY!

To keep trash out of landfills, follow the three Rs: reduce, reuse, and recycle.

BUZZ AND FLY GUY'S "THREE Rs" TIPS

1. Only buy things you really need, and use them until they wear out.

2. Bring reusable shopping bags to the store.

3. Reuse shoe boxes and cardboard for art projects or storage.

4. Reduce the amount of paper towels you use in the bathroom—you only need one to dry your hands!

5. Use a refillable container from home instead of a plastic water bottle.

6. Compost your family's food and yard waste.

7. Use clean, empty food jars to store leftovers or as mini-flowerpots.

8. Reduce how much trash you throw away by donating used clothing, toys, and electronics instead.

9. Properly recycle e-waste, metal, plastic, paper, and glass.

10. Rinse plastic and glass containers before recycling them.

Buzz and Fly Guy pledge to do their part to make our planet a better, healthier place.

"We know just what to do to reduce, reuse, and recycle!" Buzz reminded Fly Guy as they headed home.

They could not wait until their next field trip!